EXPLORATION
in History

PICTURE HISTORY

CLOTHES
EXPLORATION
FARMING
FOOD
HOMES
LANDSCAPE
MACHINERY
RECREATION
RELIGION
SCHOOLS
SHOPS
TRANSPORT
WARFARE

PICTURE HISTORY

EXPLORATION
IN HISTORY

Sheila Robertson

First published in 1984 by
Wayland (Publishers) Limited
49 Lansdowne Place, Hove
East Sussex BN3 1HF, England

© Copyright 1984 Wayland (Publishers) Ltd

ISBN 0 85078 385 2

Series Design by Behram Kapadia

Phototypeset by Kalligraphics Ltd, Redhill, Surrey
Printed in Italy by G. Canale & C.S.p.A., Turin
Bound in the U.K. by The Pitman Press, Bath

Contents

Introduction

Who was the first person to discover Europe?

It might sound a silly question. Europe has always been known; we didn't need to be discovered; this is where explorers *start* from. But the question would not sound silly to people of Asia and Africa. Although this book tells the story of European and American exploration only, we should remember that many countries 'discovered' by Europeans had a history and a culture long before the European age of exploration.

You will not fully enjoy this book unless you have an atlas in front of you while you read. Every school and library has an atlas. So should every home. Equip yourself with a map of the world and a large-scale map of whichever area you are reading about, and refer to them constantly as you read. It will help the stories come to life.

Exploration was not a mere pastime, undertaken for its own sake. Almost always it was in pursuit of influence and trade. Magellan did not sail round the world because he liked sea cruises, but to find a new route to the Spice Islands. The Conquistadors braved the unknown terrors of the New World to spread the Catholic religion and to bring back gold to their king. Brave sailors perished in the search for the North-East and North-West Passages because merchants desired a quick route to China and Japan. Exploration is always enmeshed with the history of the times.

Try hard to imagine what the explorers' conditions were like. The ship in which Christopher Columbus crossed the unknown Atlantic was only half as long again as a tennis court. When Burke and Wills were starving to death in the Australian bush they had no radio to call for aid, no helicopter rescue teams to lift them to safety, as twentieth century adventurers do.

It is important, when reading history, to try to put yourself into the minds of the people who lived at the time. Do not look at past times through a twentieth century eye. Never judge the actions of Renaissance adventurers with the views of the modern social worker. In other books you may read that Christopher Columbus tortured and hanged his own men when they defied his authority; that Vasco da Gama set fire to an Arab ship crammed with men, women, and children; that H.M. Stanley forced hundreds of people to their deaths by his burning ambition to press on through the African jungle. They were different people, living in different societies, and held different views of morality. Columbus, da Gama, and Stanley were greatly admired in their day, and deserve our admiration still for their amazing courage, vision, and achievements.

The Viking Discoveries

Vikings (or Norsemen) came from the Scandinavian countries, prowling across the North Sea in their longships, striking undefended coasts of Britain, France, and Ireland, plundering and sacking towns and, later, looking for land to colonize. This picture of a sea battle between the English and the Danes is somewhat idealized but it shows the type of ship very well. They were made of overlapping planks, and had a very shallow draught which enabled them to be landed on any handy beach. The huge square sail could only be used when going with the wind, so they needed oarsmen as well.

Iceland and Greenland

Viking ships were built for coast-hugging journeys, and were at the mercy of winds in the open ocean. So it was probably by accident that the first Viking set foot on Iceland towards the end of the eighth century. But others followed, and eventually settled there.

It was not long before this island, once an outpost, became the base for further discovery. About the year A.D. 900 an Icelander called Gunnbjorn Ulfsson was storm-swept into unknown waters. Far to the west of Iceland he caught a glimpse of a new land. No one landed there, but nearly a century later an outlaw from Norway, called Erik the Red, visited the mysterious country sighted by Ulfsson, and decided to colonize it, in the year 986. How did he find sufficient volunteers to accompany him to such a bleak, bitter, and inhospitable country? By deliberately giving the unseen country the attractive name of Greenland!

A New Continent

In 986 an Icelandic trader called Herjulfsson set out to find his father who had left with Erik the Red, but was driven far south and west by gales. When at last the sun emerged from the clouds he was completely lost. He sailed west for two more days before sighting land, and this land looked nothing like the Greenland he had been told about. It was hilly and wooded. So he turned his ship east and after four days sailing reached Greenland. What could that hilly and wooded country have been? Herjulfsson had discovered America.

Around the year 1000 Erik the Red's son, Leif Erikson, set out westwards to rediscover the land seen by Herjulfsson. He made landings in Baffin Island, Labrador, and an unidentified part of the coast which he called Vinland. After a few attempts to settle there, the visits petered out. Nevertheless, the Norsemen had beaten Columbus to the New World by nearly 500 years.

aquesta carauana es partida del imperi
de sarra panar al catayo

achion

cainu

los munts de feb
el mey los gran
fluuis G dal:

siacim

febur

facbarin

Europe's Discovery of China

In 1298 a Venetian trader named Marco Polo was taken prisoner during a sea battle between Venice and Genoa. No doubt bored during his spell in prison, he began to tell of his adventures to a fellow prisoner named Rusticiano, who was a well-known author of romantic tales. The result of this meeting was the most famous travel book ever written.

Marco's father and uncle were adventurous traders. When on the north coast of the Black Sea, war broke out and blocked their return route. While trying to get back to Venice via central Asia, they were invited to visit the court of the Great Khan. Thus they became the first Europeans ever to visit China.

Marco's First Journey

When the Polo brothers set off on their second journey to China, they took with them fifteen-year-old Marco. The picture opposite, which decorated a map of Asia made 100 years later, shows their camel caravan on its journey. They travelled through Palestine, Baghdad, up the Persian Gulf, through Persia to the Oxus River and then to the Pamir Mountains, and across the great Gobi Desert. They finally reached the Khan's court in 1275 after more than three years travelling.

The Khan took an immediate liking to the intelligent young Marco, who quickly learned the Mongol customs and language. The Khan used him as a special servant and envoy to outlying parts of his kingdom. Marco's travels took him to Yunnan, northern Burma, the borders of Tibet, Karakorum, and Vietnam, and even to India. In his seventeen years as a servant to the Khan, and in his journey to and from China, he became the widest travelled man in history up to that time.

The Polos Return

The Polo family eventually left China in 1292. They sailed by way of Sumatra, southern India, Persia, and the Black Sea port of Trebizond, returning to Venice after an absence of twenty-four years.

Marco's book of travels, written by Rusticiano, took the world by storm. Almost everything in it was new and wonderful to Europeans. Of course, some of it was disbelieved. Man-eating serpents? Stones that burned? (Few Europeans of that time had heard of alligators, and coal.)

Marco Polo was the first man who revealed to Europe the mysterious East, and tempted many others to try to follow. Among them was Christopher Columbus two hundred years later, who was inspired to find the land of China by sailing west. You can read what happened to him on page 17.

The Portuguese Venture South

Until the fifteenth century all contact between Europe and India, between East and West, was overland – through countries ruled by the great Moslem empires. The Christian Europeans did not like the Moslems having a monopoly of trade. So, about the year 1420, Prince Henry, son of King John I of Portugal, decided to do something about it.

Boiling Seas

In those days, very little was known of the west African coast. Ships had not sailed more than about a thousand miles southward. In those superstitious days, there were terrible tales of the dangers awaiting sailors who dared sail towards the unknown equator. Beyond the Canary Islands the seas were believed to boil and evaporate into treacle. Many people believed that Africa had no ending until it reached the South Pole. But Prince Henry knew that, if a way could be found round Africa, India could be reached by sea, cutting out the detested Moslems, and soon yearly expeditions were being sent southwards.

The picture opposite shows the type of ship they sailed in. They were caravels, an improved design of ship which was rigged so that it could sail close to the wind (almost into the wind).

Before Henry's first expedition set off, the southernmost limit of exploration was Cape Bojador at 26 degrees north. By Henry's death in 1460, his sailors had reached Sierra Leone at 8 degrees north, and had mapped most of West Africa's coast. Then, between 1469 and 1475, Fernão Gomes ventured along the entire 2000-mile southern coast of West Africa, and got to within 2 degrees of the equator. When he returned he was able to report that the sea had not boiled, nor turned into treacle. By 1485 another huge stride had been made with Diogo Cão reaching Cape Cross in Namibia.

Dias Reaches the Cape

In the year 1487 another sea expedition set sail southward, captained by Bartolomeo Dias. Dias tried to hug the coast after passing the mouth of the Congo, but (either accidentally through storm, or perhaps deliberately because of adverse currents and winds) at some point he stood out to sea. For many long days he sailed southwards, then decided it was time to turn east again to find the African coast and continue his southward journey. But – although he kept sailing east – he did not reach the coast. At some point during the last few days sailing he had passed the southernmost tip of Africa, and rounded the Cape.

Africa was not joined to the South Pole after all. The sea route to India was in sight.

Re-discovery of the New World

In 1492 a Genoese seaman named Christopher Columbus sailed the Atlantic. Nearly 500 years earlier, Vikings had discovered the American continent, but this was quite unknown to the rest of the world. Columbus was to rediscover it by accident, and go to his death still not believing he had found it!

Westward to the East!

By the fifteenth century most intelligent people understood that the Earth was round. Columbus became interested in the idea of reaching Asia by sailing – not east – but west across the Atlantic. His maps were based on the one made by Ptolomey in the second century. One of his outstanding errors was the belief that Asia stretched eastwards right round the world until only a short sea journey across the Atlantic separated it from Europe. Columbus became obsessed with his idea of sailing west, across the Atlantic. At last he received the support of the King of Spain. He embarked westward across the Atlantic on 3rd August 1492 with three little ships.

On 12th October they sighted land. It was only a little further from Europe than Columbus had thought. It lay at about the right latitude. It more or less agreed with Ptolomey's map. He therefore jumped ashore and gave thanks to God for having brought him to Asia. So convinced was he of this, that he ignored all the evidence to the contrary, such as primitive, brown-skinned natives, and the existence of strange plants like maize and sweet potatoes which were unheard of in Asia. He had in fact landed in the Bahamas. To this day the islands in that part of the world are called the West Indies, and the natives of America are known as Indians, because of Columbus's belief that he was in or near India.

The delightful picture opposite was drawn within a year of Columbus's landing. The artist was not a very good one, and was working only from imagination, but he tried very hard to get absolutely everything in. You can see Columbus, in his ship *Santa Maria*, and behind him the two little caravels which accompanied him. Beyond the ships is the land of China with some very strange, unChinese-looking people, trees, and tall huts with no sides. In the foreground King Ferdinand, back in Spain, is smiling benevolently on the scene, and urging Columbus onward.

An Undiscovered Ocean

Later explorers soon realized that Columbus had stumbled across a new continent, with a new ocean beyond it. The world was bigger than Ptolomey had dreamed of.

The Sea Route to India

In 1487 Dias had shown the way to the tip of Africa. Now it remained to complete the object of those explorations, which had begun seventy years before – trade with India by sea.

But let us consider, for a moment, the difficulties which lay ahead. The ships of the time were extremely slow – it would be a voyage of several months just to the Cape. After that there was still no proof that the way was clear across the ocean from Africa to India. The maps of the time, which showed India in the middle of an inland sea, might still be partly true. Finally the Moslems would be hostile, because they would not want to lose their monopoly of trade.

A Blessing on the Voyage

The man chosen to tackle these daunting difficulties was a nobleman in his late thirties called Vasco da Gama. Before departing, da Gama was summoned to King Manuel for his blessing on the voyage, as you see in this fine picture. Manuel is handing da Gama a banner consecrated by the Church. Da Gama's name can just be seen on it. By the Archbishop's feet is a map of Africa (which could not have existed ten years before). The nobleman beside the Archbishop is holding a document with Hindi writing on it, perhaps a message to the Indians they are to visit. Behind the King's dais is da Gama's caravel riding at anchor in the Tagus River.

The Portuguese Empire

Da Gama's four ships sailed in July 1497 and rounded the Cape of Good Hope in November. He sailed up the east coast of Africa until he was on the same latitude as Sierra Leone, which he had passed (on Africa's west coast) on the way south. Then he had to strike eastwards, across the unknown Indian Ocean to a point 75 degrees east. His plans soon became clear to the Moslem Arabs on the east African coast. Various difficulties were put in his way, but a little more than ten months after leaving Lisbon he arrived at the port of Calicut, on the west coast of India, the most important of the country's trading ports.

It seems a small achievement now when the journey only takes two or three weeks, but it was to have huge consequences. It opened a trading route between Europe and Asia by sea. The Mediterranean ports of Venice, Genoa, and Alexandria quickly lost their importance. The mighty Moslem empires went into decline as they lost their chief source of wealth. The Portuguese empire was soon to stretch from Brazil to the East Indies, and it was to inspire others to follow, and go further, until the whole earth was encircled.

Circumnavigation of the World

In 1518 Ferdinand Magellan, a Portuguese sailor in the service of Spain, persuaded the king to send him on an expedition to the spice-rich Moluccas Islands of Indonesia. By this time the estuary of the River Plate, in South America, had been discovered, and was believed to be a strait which led through to the unknown ocean on the other side. So Magellan would sail west, beyond the New World.

Five ships set sail in September. In December they discovered that the strait was not a strait, and had to remain on the coast of Patagonia for the winter months. In October they set sail again southwards, seeking a passage through to the far ocean. Only three days later Magellan found a real strait, the one that bears his name today, between the tip of mainland America and Tierra del Fuego. It is 320 miles long and it took him thirty-eight days to find a passage through it, never knowing if it would turn out to be just another river estuary. On sighting the broad ocean at the far end, Magellan wept for joy.

Into the Pacific Ocean

For three months he sailed west across the mighty Pacific Ocean. His crew suffered horribly from scurvy and lack of food. They ate rats, sawdust, and leather. At last they triumphantly sighted land, but only six weeks later Magellan lay dead in the Philippines, killed while unwisely helping one native ruler in a brawl against another. Our picture shows him being struck down on a beach but nobody really knows quite how he met his death. It was an inglorious end for a great man.

After many adventures, only one ship of the original five survived to return to Spain. Bearing the spices of the Moluccas, it sailed across the Indian Ocean and round South Africa, thus completing the first circumnavigation of the world.

A Pirate's Punishment

The first man to command a successful circumnavigation from beginning to end was the Englishman Francis Drake, part soldier, part pirate. Fifty-five years after Magellan's ship returned to Spain, Drake was in the Pacific plundering the Spanish shipping and towns which by now were established on South America's western coast. Knowing the Spanish would be waiting for his return he eluded them by sailing on across the Pacific, through the East Indies, round the Cape of Good Hope, and home again, bearing a huge treasure of spices and gold.

To punish him for his piracy Queen Elizabeth thought of imprisoning him, but then decided to knight him instead.

The Conquistadores

Hernando Cortez was the first of the conquistadors. After hearing that there was gold in Mexico, he sailed from the Spanish colony of Cuba in 1519. He burned his boats on the beach at Veracruz, to show his soldiers there could be no turning back. Then he marched inland to the capital of the Aztec civilization.

A Welcome for a God

He was helped by an astonishing coincidence. The Aztecs believed that their god Quetzalcoatl was due to arrive in Mexico from the Atlantic that very year. The arrival of strange white-skinned warriors, riding horses, firing their brass cannons (none of which had even been seen or heard of before) terrified them into the belief that Cortez was their returning god. The picture opposite shows him riding at the head of his army of 550 Spaniards and a few thousand native volunteers.

When the Aztec king, Montezuma, allowed the Spaniards into the city, they put him in chains. Montezuma tried to keep the peace, but was killed by his own people in an uprising. Cortez had to fight his way out of the city. In a single night he lost 450 of his own men and 4000 of the Indian allies. But just over a year later he stormed back into Tenochtitlan to destroy the city, and the Aztec civilization with it.

The story of Francisco Pizarro is very similar. After hearing of the gold and silver to be found in the land of Peru, he determined to conquer its people, the Incas. He slaughtered 10,000 of them and took their king prisoner, promising to spare his life if he filled a room with gold. The king did so. Pizarro then had him strangled. Afterwards he conquered the Peruvian capital with little difficulty, and went on to conquer and colonize the whole country.

Cruel Heroes

Neither Cortez nor Pizarro, nor the conquistadors who followed them and destroyed ancient civilizations all over central America, were conquerers only. They were inspired by Catholic zeal to convert the heathen and colonize new lands for Spain. They explored and mapped and built cities in their new domains, and added to knowledge of geography and science. They were regarded at the time as romantic adventurers and heroes. Today, (despite their extraordinary courage, imagination, and energy) we find their ruthlessness revolting, but people are entitled to be judged by the standards of their own times. Sad to say, Columbus and da Gama were also capable of dreadful cruelty, and so were later arrivals on the continent of America.

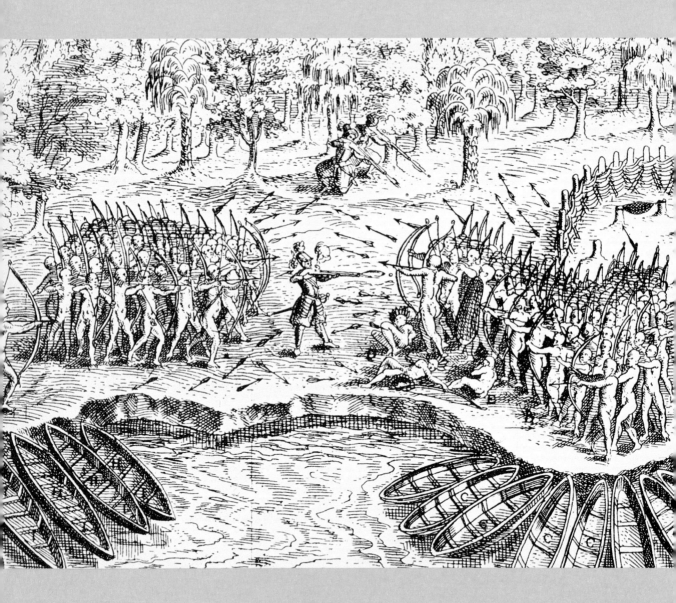

Into America

The last of the conquistadors were Hernando de Soto and Francisco Coronado, who operated north of the Gulf of Mexico in what is now the southern United States. De Soto was governor of Cuba and landed in Florida in 1539 looking for (of course) gold. He followed his quest over the Appalachian mountains and down the Alabama River. In 1541 he discovered the Mississippi.

In 1539 rumours of gold in the hinterland of New Mexico inspired another military expedition, led by Coronado. He sailed up the Gulf of California (proving that California was a peninsula) and marvelled at the great herds of buffalo he found, and the copper-skinned Indians who followed them. One of his detachments discovered the Grand Canyon, and Coronado himself reached present-day Kansas. Of course the expedition was written off as a hopeless failure, because it discovered no gold.

Discovery of Manhattan

It was an Englishman named Henry Hudson, in the service of the Dutch East India Company, who gave the Dutch a foothold in the New World. In 1613, excited by the furs that Hudson had brought back, Dutch traders reached the river Hudson had discovered (which was one day to bear his name). They built a trading post and a fort on Manhattan Island. Over the next few years trappers made their way up the Hudson and Mohawk rivers, and it was not long before they discovered another great river, which seemed to lead forever westward. Could this be the long-sought route to the far Pacific? But they were not to find out, for the river was the St Lawrence, and it was already controlled by the French.

Indian Allies

How had the French managed to outflank the Spanish and the Dutch? It was Samuel de Champlain who, between 1603 and 1615, claimed control of the vast region spreading from Nova Scotia in the east to Lake Superior in the west. He had set himself the task of opening up this huge and rich area to the French fur traders. He befriended the Algonquin and Huron Indians, and learned methods of travel from them. He even helped them in their tribal wars. Opposite, you can see him helping to defeat their Iroquois rivals, in a skirmish of 1609, on the edge of the lake now named after him. Champlain and his men had guns, which the Iroquois had never seen. But everything has its price. Later, when the English and French were fighting for mastery in the region, the English found in the Iroquois their natural allies.

The North-west Passage

As soon as Europeans discovered a continent standing in the way of their westward route to Asia, they started to look for a way round it, and so began the centuries-long search for a passage between the continent and the North Pole.

The first such expedition was only four years after Columbus reached the New World. In June 1497 Giovanni Cabot, a Venetian in the service of Henry VII of England, sighted Nova Scotia, He was therefore the first discoverer of the American mainland since the Vikings, for Columbus had only reached the West Indies at the time, and did not touch the mainland until 1498.

The Death of Hudson

In 1576 the Englishman Martin Frobisher sailed past the southern tip of Greenland to reach Baffin Island. The Mongoloid features of the Eskimos made him believe he had reached Asia!

In this picture we see some of Frobisher's crew who have taken one of the ship's boats to explore a narrow inlet. In the foreground is a large kayak (Eskimo canoe) and there are several more in the background. Frobisher's men are being attacked with bows and arrows.

Other English expeditions followed, and in 1610 Henry Hudson entered the strait between Labrador and Baffin Island and eventually found himself at the entrance to what seemed a mighty ocean. Had he turned north he would have been well on the way to discovering a north-west passage, but he coasted southwards, deep into a bay. In November his ship became stuck fast in the ice, and his crew mutinied. With a few men (including his young son) Hudson was cruelly set adrift in an open boat, and never seen again.

In 1615 William Baffin sailed through the strait Hudson had found, and as far north as Smith Sound. In 1829, James Clark Ross was icebound for three years on the Boothian Peninsula.

The Search for Franklin

In 1825–7 John Franklin continued the search from the Canadian hinterland. He sailed down the Mackenzie river to its mouth, then traced the coast westwards to meet another expedition sailing east from Bering Strait. They got to within 160 miles of each other. Twenty years later Franklin sailed into Baffin Bay and was never seen again. In the next nine years no fewer than fifteen expeditions went searching for him, but without success.

In 1906 the *Gjoa*, under the Norwegian Roald Amundsen, became the first single ship to sail the whole length of the North-west Passage.

Across Canada

While the conqueror Pizarro was rampaging around Peru, the Frenchman, Jacques Cartier, was quietly making voyages of exploration up the St Lawrence river, thousands of miles to the north. And while Pizarro was destroying a country, Cartier was taking the first steps to create one, for it was he who gave Canada its name. Hearing a similar word used to describe an Indian village, he applied it to the whole country.

Down the Mississippi

A century later, other Frenchmen extended knowledge of Canada increasingly westward beyond the Great Lakes. Then Robert Cavelier, Sieur de la Salle, made a voyage down the Mississippi. He had a dream of extending French influence southwards to the Gulf of Mexico. At the mouth of the Mississippi he named the region Louisiana in honour of the French King Louis XIV.

The first man to cross Canada to the Pacific Ocean was Alexander Mackenzie, a Scots-Canadian. He was an employee of the North-West Company of Canada, a rival to the Hudson's Bay Company. With a small party of men he sailed up the Peace and Parsnip rivers, canoeing and portaging, until he reached the great range of mountains which ran down the entire western edge of the American continent. For most of their length they are named the Rocky Mountains.

A first Sight of the Pacific

Mackenzie's band managed to cross the Rockies as far as the Frazer river. He thought this would lead them to the sea, but friendly Indians warned him that it was too difficult a journey. He then explored further south, and at last found the Bellacoola river which carried him to his destination. On a rock at Puget Sound he proudly wrote his name, 'Alex Mackenzie', and added 'from Canada by land 22d July 1793'.

On the opposite page you can see an artist's impression of the scene as Mackenzie and his little band of adventurers arrived on the shore of the Pacific. Mackenzie, as leader, still manages to look like a European, but the others look more like Indians. They have adopted several articles of Indian dress. Their scarves, which began the journey round their necks, are now used as headbands to hold back their long, greasy hair. One has a tomahawk stuck in his belt. Their clothes are almost worn away.

Mackenzie's book about his journey was read by Thomas Jefferson, the President of the United States. Inspired by the idea of overland crossings, he organized one of his own, which we shall read about in the next chapter.

Crossing the Rockies

In 1783 the eastern states of the American colonies gained their independence from Britain and became the United States of America. However, large parts of the country still belonged to France, Spain, and Mexico. In 1803 the U.S.A. – by buying Louisiana from France – nearly doubled the size of its territory.

Much of this territory was virtually unknown. Thus, the following year, an expedition started westwards with the intention of finding out just what the country had acquired, and of discovering new routes to the Pacific.

A Winter with the Indians

The leaders of this expedition were Meriwether Lewis and William Clark. They spent the winter of 1804–5 on the Missouri, 1,600 miles from St Louis. They built huts, and lived with the Mandan Indians. In the spring they set off again, following the Missouri river until they reached its source in the snow-capped Rockies. In September they reached the Columbia river, built canoes, and floated downriver to the Pacific Ocean. This expedition planted the first signposts to the American West.

Hard on the heels of Lewis and Clark, fur trappers and hunters entered the Rocky Mountains. They were looking mainly for beaver, whose pelts fetched high prices back in the east. It was the trappers and the traders who did the main job of opening up the far west to those who followed.

Along the Santa Fe Trail

After a war with Mexico, the United States was left in possession of Texas, New Mexico, and California. This began a great westward wave of emigration towards California. Whole families with their furniture and livestock crammed into horse- and ox-drawn wagons followed the trails blazed by the explorers. Now the trappers and hunters and traders turned to guiding the emigrants. The picture you see opposite is typical of dozens of scenes of the 1830s and 1840s. A lone mountain man, alert for hostile Indians, leads another hopeful party to a new life in the west. A line of ox-drawn covered wagons snakes out behind him for a mile over the prairie. They carry men mainly, but also women and even children. There were no roads or even paths across the treeless plains, alkali deserts, and formidable mountain ranges. There was just the occasional blazed tree-stump, the debris of a previous expedition, a word of help from a friendly Indian.

The discovery of new routes, and the settling of new areas, by the dauntless emigrants, completed the exploration and discovery of western America.

The North-east Passage

Henry Hudson has already appeared twice in this book. He discovered the Hudson river on which New York now stands, and pioneered the search for the North-west Passage. However, before either of these exploits, he had already made three journeys in search of a north-*east* passage to the Pacific.

Hudson's first two attempts were unsuccessful, and when the weather made his third mission impossible he turned about to seek the north-west passage instead.

Early Maps

In 1594 William Barents was commissioned by Dutch merchants to explore north and east of Norway. He rounded Norway, set course eastward, and arrived at the huge, long island of Novaya Zemlya, lying like a 600-mile crescent across his path. Failing to sail round it to the north, he returned to Amsterdam. The following year he tried and failed again.

For his third attempt he decided to steer a more northerly course to avoid the difficulties of the Novaya Zemlya coast. He discovered Bear Island, then sailed east and successfully rounded the northern tip of the great island obstacle. But on the east coast the ice closed in, held the ship fast, and crushed it. The men trudged ashore, salvaging what they could from the wreck. With no hope of rescue, they built a hut with the timbers of the ship. There it is in the picture. The strange, central tower is the crow's nest from the top of the ship's mast. There they settled down to the worst winter ever endured by Europeans, a bare 12 degrees from the North Pole. Even in the hut, with a fire in the middle of the room, the sheets froze on their beds, and the drink in their glasses.

What did they do to while away those long, weary months? Barents' mission had been to reach China. So, with amazing single-mindedness, he read aloud to his men from a book called *A History and Description of the Great Chinese Empire*. However, when the spring finally came, they knew it was impossible for them to continue the journey. In mid-June 1595, they embarked in their longboats for the mainland 1600 miles away, but Barents died after five days. The sea between Spitzbergen and Novaya Zemlya is named after him.

The Passage is Found

The North-east Passage was finally conquered by Nils Nordenskiold, a Swede born in Finland. Between June 1878 and September 1879, in his ship *Vega*, he successfully completed the journey from the Atlantic to the Pacific along the north coast of Asia.

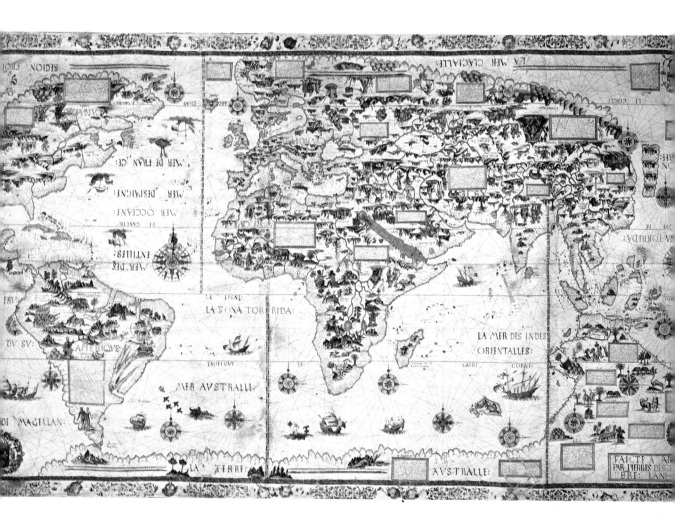

34

Terra Australis Incognita

By 1550, when this map was drawn, da Gama had rounded Africa, the New World had been discovered, and Magellan had sailed around the southern tip of the American continent. Europeans had mapped all the coasts of the New World except the north-west, and had a reasonably accurate idea of the geography of the Far East. Yet there were still two vast continents to be discovered, and another – even vaster – to be eliminated from maps like this.

An Imaginary Continent

For more than ten centuries people had assumed that, because there was so much land in the northern hemisphere, there must be an equal amount in the southern hemisphere, to 'balance the globe'. In their minds, and on their maps, they placed it in the only unexplored sea left – the Southern Ocean. They gave it the name of Unknown Land (which in Latin is Terra Incognita) or Unknown South Land (Terra Australis Incognita). On this map you can see a strip of a huge continent running right across the bottom until it reaches the longitude of India, then swinging north-east to join up with the more or less discovered parts of the East Indies and beyond. It is a French map so the continent has a French name: La Terre Australle.

Tierra del Fuego, at the tip of South America, is a part of this supposed continent. When Magellan had rounded the world he had sailed through the straits between Tierra del Fuego and the mainland. No one knew there was open sea to the south of Tierra del Fuego until Drake sailed in those waters in 1578.

Discovery of a Myth

Buried in this imagined continent was a real one: the one we today call Australia. In the early seventeenth century, Dutch sailors made landfalls on Australia's north-west coast, and named it New Holland. They had no idea how far this land extended, however.

In 1768 a British Navy captain, James Cook, set sail across the Pacific with instructions to find Terra Australis. He circumnavigated both islands of New Zealand, proving they were not part of Australia. Then he touched upon the south-east shore of Australia, probably the first European to do so, and named it New South Wales. On a second expedition from 1772 to 1775 he sailed from Cape Town across a part of the Antarctic Circle to a point off southern New Zealand, 71 degrees south, and at last proved to everyone's satisfaction that Terra Australis Incognita was a myth.

The way was now clear for the exploration of the last continent (Antarctica).

The Dutch in the East

In 1580 Portugal became a province of Spain. Their spice trade declined, and the Dutch sailed in to take it over.

Discovery of New Holland

With so many ships sailing eastward from the Cape of Good Hope, it was only a matter of time before one of them overshot the East Indies and reached the north-western shore of Australia. This first happened in about 1605, and by 1627 Dutch sea-captains, looking for more spice territories, had rounded the western cape and sailed eastwards for 1000 miles along the Great Australian Bight. They called this unexplored territory New Holland.

In 1642 Antony Van Diemen, governor-general of the East Indies Company, ordered Abel Janszoon Tasman to explore the seas south of New Holland and take possession of any territory he found. Tasman sailed from Mauritius in October 1642, crossed the Indian Ocean, and continued eastward between the latitudes of 44 and 47 degrees east. On 24th November he sighted land, and in honour of the governor-general he named it Van Diemen's Land (now Tasmania). But Tasman was not the stuff of which explorers are made. He did not make a landing to inspect the country, and soon sailed on eastward.

Nine days later he sighted the south island of New Zealand, but it only took a little skirmish with the Maoris from their boats to deter him from landing there either. He sailed north to Fiji, and back home to Batavia via the well-known northern coast of New Guinea. Thus he managed to circumnavigate the huge landmass of Australia without ever seeing it!

Van Diemen criticized Tasman for not trying hard enough. Nevertheless in 1644 he ordered him out again, to search for a strait between New Guinea and New Holland. Tasman contented himself with exploring the southern coast of New Guinea, sailing into the Gulf of Carpentaria, then coasting back westwards. To Van Diemen it seemed caution bordering on cowardice, and Tasman was not sent out again.

Tasman's Own Drawings

The pictures opposite are taken from Tasman's own journal. They show the friendly natives of the Tonga and Fiji Islands. Tasman's sketches are quite skilful, and show exactly what the outrigger canoes looked like, as well as the larger sailing craft. In the upper picture women and men are bringing fruit to the beach, and men can be seen swimming towards the Dutch ships, pushing their fruit ahead of them on wooden trays, to sell it to the sea-weary sailors.

Across Australia

In 1859 the South Australian government offered a prize to the first person to cross the continent from south to north, a vast distance of 2000 miles. There were two contenders – John McDouall Stuart and Robert O'Hara Burke.

Stuart set out in January 1860 with only two companions on horseback. By April they had reached the centre of the continent, and planted the British flag there. Lack of water, and hostile aborigines, prevented them going much further, and at the end of June Stuart was forced to turn back.

Seven months after Stuart, Burke set off on his attempt. He had eighteen men mounted on horses and camels. He started from Menindie on the Darling river with his advance party, and quickly covered the first stage of the journey to Cooper Creek. But Burke became too impatient for the rest of the party to catch up, and set off impetuously for the north with his second in command, W. J. Wills and only two others. The rest of his expedition were left behind leaderless.

First Across the Continent

Burke dashed in a straight line, disregarding water-courses, but was lucky enough to have an exceptionally wet season, and found water all the way. In almost any other year such a route would have killed them within weeks. Even so, it was full of hardship, and our picture shows a typical scene of their journey. The party did actually succeed in reaching the northern coast, in January 1861, but on the return journey their food and their strength ran out, and all but one of them died. Reckless and incompetent as the expedition had been, nevertheless it is to them that the honour of being first belongs.

Stuart Tries Again

Meanwhile, in November 1860, Stuart had made a second attempt, which again failed. Nevertheless, in October 1861, before news of Burke's triumph and disaster had reached him, he set off on his third determined effort. Nine months after his departure from Adelaide, Stuart proudly raised the Union Jack at Chambers Bay in July 1862.

Stuart was a prudent explorer, as brave as Burke, but more intelligent, and with a vision of those to follow him. At the coast he had written in his diary, 'I hope this may be the first sign of the dawn of approaching civilization.' Indeed it was. The great age of Australian exploration was soon to cover the continent. And within ten years of Stuart's return the overland telegraph line from Adelaide to Darwin was opened along the trail which Stuart had blazed.

The Frozen North

Fridtjof Nansen, of Norway, did not believe the Arctic was a continent. He believed it was a huge, icebound ocean, perpetually on the move. He built a ship specially designed so that the ice could not crush it. His daring plan was to let the ship become frozen in the ice, then allow the ocean currents to carry it drifting across the Pole.

Sailing in June 1893, the ship became locked in the ice in September. For six months they drifted in the Arctic night – but westwards, not north. Nansen therefore resolved to make a dash for the Pole on foot, and set off with one companion and dogs, sledges, and kayaks.

A Winter in the Arctic

By April, having reached further north than anyone in history, he was forced to abandon the attempt and they retreated southwards to Franz Josef Land. In September 1896 they built a stone hut roofed with walrus skins, and sat out the winter until the following May. They finally arrived back in Norway in August 1897, after long being given up for dead.

At about the same time Robert Peary, an American naval officer, was also trying to reach the Pole. Peary was a man obsessed with the desire to be first, to leave his name in history. Between 1886 and 1906 he led seven expeditions to the Arctic, surveying routes, and studying the ways of the Eskimos. Back home in the States he divided his time between writing books about his adventures, and raising funds for the next one. On many of his expeditions he was accompanied by his remarkable wife, Josephine, who gave birth to her daughter Marie whilst exploring within the Arctic Circle.

Peary's Eighth Attempt

In 1908 Peary seemed to understand that he was being given his last chance. There had been many failures. He was now fifty-two years old. He sailed from Ellesmere Island to his advance base at Cape Columbia, with fifty Eskimos, 250 dogs, and, as always, his black servant and companion, Matthew Henson. At times the ice parted and left them faced with water channels. Pressure ridges of ice, up to fifty feet high, had to be climbed, and the sledges hauled up. On one occasion they crossed a quarter-mile wide channel on a succession of ice floes. At last Peary led the final assault with Henson and four Eskimos. After five days' forced march, he unfurled the American flag at the North Pole on 7th April 1909.

Here is the photograph he took on that occasion, of Ooqueah, Ootah, Henson, Egingwah, and Seegloo. They are standing in front of a pressure ridge about three miles from the Pole.

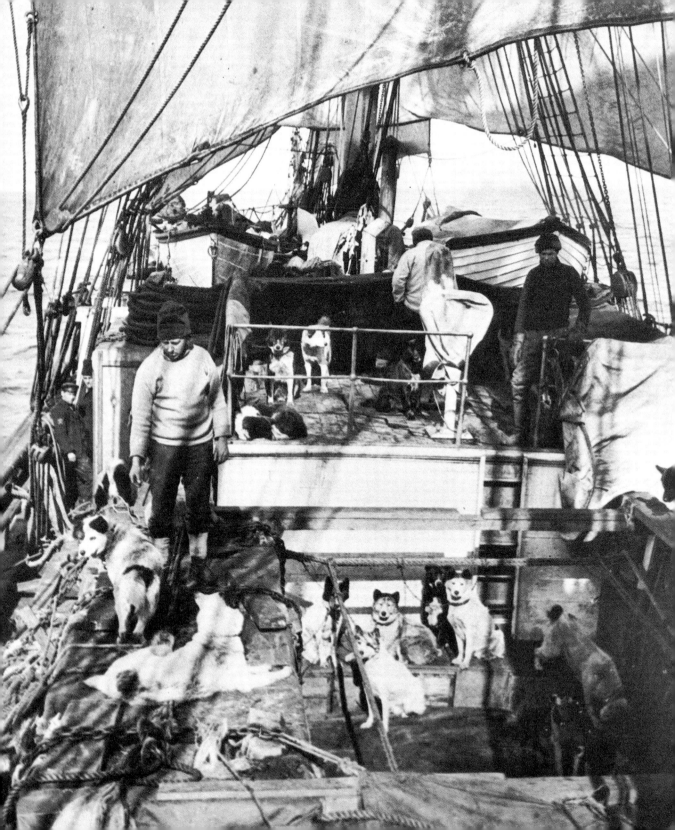

The Race to the South Pole

Captain Cook circumnavigated the continent of Antarctica, but without ever actually seeing it. Sixty-five years later, in 1839, James Clark Ross, whom we last saw looking for the North-west Passage, page 27, spent three years in the Antarctic and reached a latitude that was not overtaken for another sixty years.

Then on to the scene came the Norwegian Roald Amundsen. In 1906 he had captained the first ship to sail completely through the North-west Passage. His next ambition was to reach the North Pole, but when Peary beat him to it he switched his sights from one end of the earth to the other. At that time Britain was mounting an expedition, captained by Robert Falcon Scott, to reach the South Pole. Amundsen decided to make a race of it. Sportingly he sent a telegram to Scott to warn him that the race was on.

Eight Weeks to the Pole

Amundsen reached the Antarctic, set up camp in the Bay of Whales, and began his assault in October, with only four companions. He had four sledges and fifty-two dogs. Exactly eight weeks later his party stood triumphantly at the Pole.

Here you see Scott's ship, *Terra Nova*, *en route* for the Antarctic from Melbourne. Scattered all over the deck, lying in odd corners, in gangways, and on piles of rope, are the husky dogs on which all polar expeditions depend. As you can see, it is still the age of sail, and life was a little primitive in other ways too. There are none of the concentrated rations, lightweight clothing, and inflatable tents with which modern expeditions travel. And, of course, no radio on which to call for help in emergency.

Death in the Snow

The British party started for the Pole two weeks behind Amundsen, from sixty miles further north, and burdened with the snow tractors and Siberian ponies Scott had insisted on bringing. In the event they proved useless to him. Even the dogs were not properly trained, and eventually the men had to take over the hauling of the sledges themselves. After a harder journey than Amundsen's, the five men of the final assault party reached the Pole on 17th January, only to see the Norwegian flag fluttering there. It must have been a moment of bitter disappointment. Sick at heart they began to retrace their steps, but were now troubled with scurvy and frostbite. One man collapsed and died. Another bravely committed suicide rather than hold up the others. Eventually the other three collapsed from exhaustion and died when only eleven miles from a supply depot.

The Source of the Nile

Since history began, the Nile had continued to roll out of the African continent, flooding its Egyptian banks in the driest season of the year. Yet no expedition to discover where it came from had ever achieved its object. In 1856 two Englishmen – Richard Burton and John Speke – determined to find the answer.

A Bitter Quarrel

With more than 100 porters, and provisions for two years, they struck inland from the east African coast for five months until, 900 miles from their starting point, they reached Lake Tanganyika. By this time both men were ill, but when Speke recovered he trekked 200 miles northward and found another great lake, which he named Victoria. Burton strongly believed Tanganyika was the source. Speke hotly insisted it was Victoria.

Arriving back in Britain first, Speke claimed for himself the discovery of the source of the Nile. He was greeted with amazed delight, and immediately the Royal Geographical Society raised the money for a further expedition. This time Speke was to be accompanied by James Grant. In all the excitement, Burton and his alternative theory were completely overlooked.

After a two-year journey, Speke stood again at the edge of the lake he had named Victoria. This time he was on the southern shore, and watched a river tumbling over a mighty falls and flowing away to the south. Convinced now that Lake Victoria was indeed the source of the Nile, he marched down to Egypt and thence home again, to the acclamation of the Royal Geographical Society. He had named the falls the Ripon Falls, after the president of the society. There he stands in the picture opposite, together with other senior members of the society, listening with respectful interest as Speke and Grant deliver a lecture to its members. The map of Africa behind them on the wall, made, of course, before their discovery, is necessarily vague in detail. The date is 22nd June 1863.

Another Mystery

But Burton challenged his findings. Some geographers sided with Burton, some with Speke. Eventually a debate between Burton and Speke was organized at Bath. On the morning of the debate, Speke killed himself while out shooting partridges. Was it an accident, or was it suicide?

Other expeditions were sent up the Nile, and slowly the truth began to emerge. Speke was right and Burton was wrong. Lake Victoria is the source of the Nile.

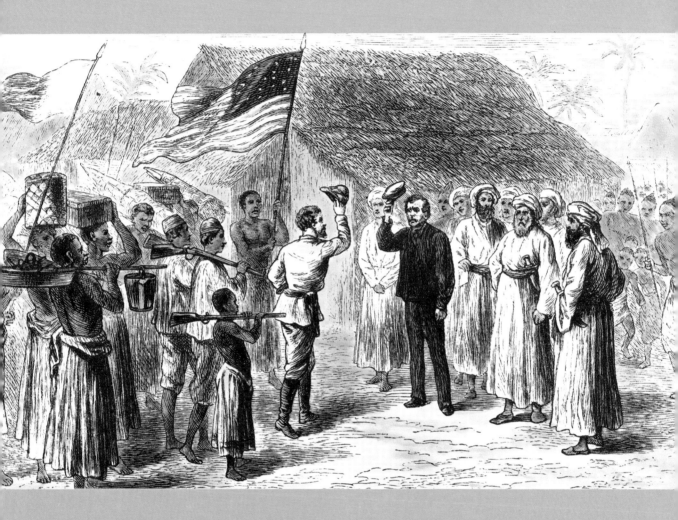

Darkest Africa

By the nineteenth century much of Africa, though relatively unexplored, was not exactly a mystery to Europeans. Adequate maps existed of the Moslem north, and large areas of South Africa had been settled by Europeans. It was central Africa – darkest Africa as it was called, the vast area lying largely between the Congo in the north and the Zambesi in the south – which was still a white space on the map.

Many explorers ventured into this vast and comfortless region. Two of the most colourful were the Scotsman David Livingstone, and Henry Morton Stanley, an American.

A Famous Meeting

Sent to South Africa as a missionary, the lust for exploration soon assumed a greater importance in Livingstone's mind.

In 1866 he was invited to settle the great argument still raging about the source of the Nile. He spent five long and miserable years of travel, getting weaker all the time with malaria and dysentery. In November 1871 he was camped on the shore of Lake Tanganyika when a white man stepped out of the bush, shook his hand, and uttered the most famous words in the history of exploration.

'Dr Livingstone, I presume.'

The man was H. M. Stanley. Born in Wales, he ran away from the workhouse, went to sea as a cabin boy, was adopted by a kindly American from whom he took his name and nationality, fought on both sides in the American Civil War, then became a journalist. He already had a great reputation as a reporter when his newspaper sent him, largely as a publicity stunt, to look for David Livingstone.

The Source of the Congo

Stanley set off from Zanzibar in March 1871 and arrived at the town of Ujiji on Lake Tanganyika eight months later. By an extraordinary stroke of luck, Livingstone had recently arrived there from the Lualaba river. Livingstone died fifteen months after the famous meeting, and Stanley decided to complete the work Livingstone had left unfinished.

Stanley was the greatest and most successful of all explorers in Africa. By May 1875 he had settled the truth about Lake Victoria. Fifteen months later he sailed right round Lake Tanganyika and proved once and for all that it was not the source of the Nile. But the greatest adventure, an epic of exploration, was his journey down the mysterious Lualaba, which he discovered to be in fact the Congo, down to the Atlantic.

The blank space on the map was a blank no longer. Darkest Africa had been brought into the light.

The Lure of the Desert

In the Moslem north of Africa lies the world's best-known desert, the Sahara. Many Europeans, lured by the mysterious and once-proud city of Timbuktu on the upper Niger, on the southern fringe of the desert, have tried to cross the burning miles of desert sand from the north, or the tropical forests and high scrub land from the south and west.

Timbuktu and Back

The greatest of Saharan travellers was the German, Heinrich Barth. He was the first European to have been more interested in the history of the region and the customs of its people, than in the glory of his own exploits in discovering them. He spent five years travelling and studying along the southern fringe of the Sahara between Lake Chad and Timbuktu, and made reliable maps of huge areas of Africa.

In the harsh deserts of Arabia itself, the greatest lure has been the forbidden cities of Mecca and Medina. Arabs disliked Christians being in their country at all, and no one, unless they were of the Moslem faith, were permitted to enter the holy cities. Yet a number of amazingly brave and resourceful Europeans have done it.

The first was John Lewis Burckardt, a Swiss. He studied the Arabic language and religion, then disguised himself as an Arab and travelled through the Middle East to Cairo. He hoped to cross the Sahara to the source of the Niger. Unable to do so, he went into Nubia and joined an annual pilgrimage to Mecca. Once on this journey he was suspected of being an infidel, and to put it to the test he was examined in a knowledge of the Koran. Not only did he convince his examiners that he was a devout Moslem, but he was proclaimed to be a great Koranic scholar!

Travelling in Disguise

Our picture shows the desert camp of another daring scholar and adventurer, Richard Burton. He became fluent in more than thirty languages, and enjoyed disguising himself and travelling unsuspected among natives of India and Arabia. In 1853, disguised as an Afghan pilgrim, he made the journey to both Mecca and Medina.

Two years later he entered another forbidden holy city – Harar in Ethiopia. This painting is by a companion on that journey. It shows the black tents of the Bedouin Arabs, and the camels which are the main transport in the desert. Notice how the guy-lines of the tents are weighted with stones, for there was no hold for pegs in that shifting sand. Burton is probably in the picture somewhere, if you can see through his disguise.

The Forbidden East

Several parts of the world have been forbidden to foreigners. For centuries Japan was a closed country. Large parts of the Moslem world were also forbidden territory, and Christian explorers there risked death for their curiosity. Perhaps the most mysterious of all these places was the mountain fastness of Tibet, in central Asia.

The Forbidden City

The first well-known European to try to force his way to the forbidden city of Lhasa, Tibet's capital, was the Russian soldier Nikolay Przhevalsky. In 1870 he began a journey deep into central Asia from Lake Baikal on the border with Mongolia, crossed the Gobi Desert, and entered Tibet by way of Kalgan. But winter was upon him, and 500 miles from Lhasa he had to turn back. On later journeys he discovered the primitive wild Mongolian horse which is now named after him, and got to within 200 miles of Lhasa before being turned back.

In 1901 and 1906 a Swedish diplomat named Sven Hedin made two determined attempts to enter Tibet disguised as a Mongol, but was discovered and turned back.

Neither of these great explorers ever saw the Potala Palace of Lhasa. It was built in the seventeenth century on the ruins of a fortress erected by the ancient kings of Tibet. It is the palace of Tibet's supreme religious ruler, the Dalai Lama. It is also a monastery served by hundreds of monks of the Buddhist religion. Very few non-Tibetans have ever seen it. Even fewer have gone inside.

Across the Himalayas

Two Europeans who did see it, however, were Austrian mountaineers who escaped from a British internment camp in India and walked across the Himalayas into Tibet. It is one of the most incredible stories of this century.

Heinrich Harrer and Peter Aufschnaiter had been mountain-climbing in India when the Second World War broke out. The British colonial power interned them. In 1943 they escaped from their internment camp at Dehra Dun, climbed the Himalayan passes, crossed the Chanthang plateau, ascended Mount Nyenchenthanglka, and finally reached the Forbidden City. For a well-equipped expedition it would have been a proud accomplishment. For two travellers, without proper equipment or even clothing (Harrer did not even have gloves for the temperature of 40 degrees below zero) it was almost unbelievable. Eventually they stayed in Tibet for seven years, made friends with the young god-king, the Dalai Lama, and accompanied him on his flight to India when the Chinese invaded in 1950.

The Voyage of the Kon-Tiki

When the first Europeans crossed the Pacific – by far the mightiest of the oceans – they discovered right in the middle of it a number of small, mountainous islands, many thousands of miles from the nearest mainland. To their astonishment, every one of these islands was inhabited by people of the same race – civilized people who grew corn, bred animals, and built houses and temples. On some islands there were paved roads, old pyramids, and statues as high as a four-storey building.

By Raft Across the Pacific

Where had these people come from? The question puzzled people for four centuries. Then in 1937 a Norwegian naturalist and anthropologist named Thor Heyerdahl set out to find the answer. He became convinced that the people of these Polynesian islands had drifted across the Pacific from South America on rafts, in two great waves of emigration, about 1400 and 800 years ago. When nobody would believe that a journey of such a huge distance could be made on a raft, he built one of his own, and with five companions and one parrot set sail on the afternoon of 28th April 1947, from the Peruvian bay of Callao.

The raft is shown opposite. It is modelled after those of the Indians of Peru some hundreds of years ago. It has a square sail hung from a pair of masts lashed together, a small open cabin behind it, and a long steering oar at the stern. It is made of nine huge balsa logs lashed together with rope, with small balsa logs laid across them. The deck and walls of the cabin are made of bamboo, and the cabin is roofed with banana leaves. There are no nails, wire, or metal in the construction. All the logs and planks are held together with ropes, in faithful imitation of the ancient Peruvian craft. The size of the vessel is 45 × 18 feet, which means that five small cars could have fitted along its length, but only two across the width.

Their voyage took them 4300 miles, drifting ever westward in the Humboldt Current of the Pacific. They had to learn how to steer and sail the raft only after they set out. They had encounters with whales and sharks, and became adept at catching fish and small dolphins.

On 21st July, 101 days after their departure, they grounded on a reef on the island of Raroia.

Proof for a Theory

Heyerdahl had proved his point. American Indians could have peopled the Polynesian islands by drifting on rafts across the Pacific. But he could not prove they actually had done so, for there are many mysteries still to explain.

The Roof of the World

The highest range of mountains in the world lies along the south-western border of Tibet, extending northwards through Kashmir and Pakistan. The Himalayas contain dozens of the world's highest peaks, and the highest of them all is Mount Everest at 29,028 feet.

Modern mountaineering had begun in the Alps in the middle of the nineteenth century. Before long, however, there were no virgin peaks left.

First to the Top

By the early 1950s, several parties had reached to within 1,000 feet of Everest's summit. But the last 1,000 feet are by far the hardest; they were further from success than the distance indicates. Many people believe that George Mallory and Andrew Irvine reached the summit before disappearing without trace on a 1924 expedition – certainly they must have got within 200 feet. But the eventual success went to Edmund Hillary of New Zealand and Tenzing Norgay of Nepal on the 1953 British Expedition.

The photograph opposite shows Tenzing standing proudly on the peak, with flags fluttering from his ice-axe in the frozen wind nearly six miles high. Hillary said, in his book *High Adventure*, 'The thought drifted through my mind that this photograph should be a good one if it came out at all . . . I took three pictures of Tenzing on the summit (hoping that one would come out)'.

News of the magnificent climb reached Britain on the coronation day of Queen Elizabeth II, and set the crowds cheering along the route. 'Which man actually reached the top first?' demanded the world's press (and even some politicians). Their reply was, 'We reached it together on the same rope'.

Taming of the Himalayas

This did not, however, mean the end of Himalayan exploration. Successful climbs of Everest have been made by teams of several countries since, and all the greatest Himalayan peaks were conquered during the following ten years. K2, the world's second highest mountain at 28,250 feet, was scaled by an Italian party in 1954. In 1955 a French party succeeded in getting all its members to the top of Makalu (27,790 feet, the world's fifth highest). In the same year a British team climbed Kanchenjunga (28,168 feet, the third highest). Lhotse, the world's fourth highest peak at 27,890 feet, was climbed by a Swiss team in 1956.

The greatest peaks of the world have now been climbed, but in the Himalayas there are still dozens of others awaiting the courage and determination of explorers who climb among mountains.

Man Reaches the Moon

In 1903 a pair of American bicycle manufacturers built an aeroplane which flew for twelve seconds, and the history of space travel had begun. Six years later a Frenchman flew an aeroplane across the English Channel. The first rocket to use liquid fuel was launched by a lone American amateur in 1928. In 1944 a German rocket reached 118 miles above the earth. Thirteen years later a Russian satellite (an artificial moon) was placed into orbit around the earth. A few months later another one went up, carrying the first traveller in space – a dog named Laika.

First man in Space

Laika was followed in 1961 by a young Russian Air Force pilot named Yuri Gagarin. On 12th April he circumnavigated the world just once in 108 minutes (Drake had taken 147 weeks), and no one now doubted that one day man would travel in space.

In fact that day was not far off. Americans began to make satellite launches, unmanned landings on the moon, and link-ups in space between two vehicles each carrying a crew. The first American astronaut orbited the Earth in February 1962, the year in which a young man named Neil Armstrong began his training as an astronaut. He was eventually selected as commander of the crew of three men (Armstrong, Michael Collins, and Buz Aldrin) on the Apollo 11 mission to land on the moon.

That day millions of people sat glued to their T.V. sets to watch the most extraordinary adventure in history. The spaceship entered the moon's gravity and went into orbit around it. Whilst Collins stayed in the command ship encircling the moon, Armstrong and Aldrin entered the lunar module and descended towards the area named long ago as the Sea of Tranquillity. Armstrong stepped out on to the surface, and announced, in words that rang across space: 'A small step for a man: a great leap for mankind'.

The End of Exploration

That marked the end of the history of exploration. There is nothing left to 'explore' in the old sense. No one will ever again set off into the unknown, not knowing what he will find. Teams of rigorously trained scientists, backed by thousands of technicians, administered by politicians, and with millions of T.V. 'live' spectators, will depart the earth and enter upon new worlds. But one can't help feeling sad that brave, eccentric individuals, inspired by courage, curiosity, and pride, and with no idea of what they may find, will never again set off on a lonely route into the unknown.

Acknowledgements and Sources of Pictures

cover A painting by an artist unknown to the publishers reproduced by permission of Afrikaner Library, Univeristy of The Witwatersrand, Johannesburg.

page 10 A painting by Colin Gill (1892–1940) recoloured for its appearance in this book. (Crown Copyright: reproduced with permission of the Controller, H.M. Stationery Office)

page 12 An illustration from the Catalan Map, done on parchment in 1375 for Charles V of France. It shows the Polo family's expedition on its way from Bokhara to Peking. (Wayland Picture Library)

page 14 This woodcut was taken from an edition of *The Nuremberg Chronicles* first published in 1493. It illustrates the building of the Ark, from the Genesis story in the Bible, but in fifteenth-century style. After the picture was drawn, it was copied on to a block of wood by cutting away the parts not required. The outline was then inked and pressed on to the paper. The engraving has been coloured for its appearance in this book. (The Mansell Collection)

page 16 An unknown contemporary artist's impression of Columbus's journey to the New World, which probably appeared in an early sixteenth-century book. It has been coloured for its appearance in this book. (Wayland Picture Library)

page 18 This picture also appears on the cover, and is described above.

page 20 An engraving, probably for an early nineteenth-century book; coloured for its appearance here. (Wayland Picture Library)

page 22 A Spanish panel painting on wood completed in 1698, and kept at the Museum de America in Madrid. It shows Cortez riding to meet Montezuma. (The Bridgeman Art Library)

page 24 A contemporary line engraving probably taken from a book, showing the battle in 1609 between Indian tribes in which Champlain sided with the Algonquins and Hurons against the Iroquois. (Photo Research International)

page 26 A watercolour entitled 'Englishmen in a skirmish with Eskimos' from the Sloane Album at the British Museum. It is a contemporary copy of a picture by John White, who accompained Walter Raleigh to Virginia, and there is some doubt as to whether it depicts an incident of the Frobisher expedition. (Wayland Picture Library)

page 28 'Mackenzie at the Pacific' painted by Charles William Jefferys (1869–1952). (Picture Division, Public Archives, Ottawa)

page 30 'When Wagon Trails Were Dim' painted by Charles M Russell, known as the Cowboy Artist from having been a cowboy in Montana. (Peter Newark's Western Americana)

page 32 This drawing was probably done by a member of Barents' expedition, who actually helped to build the hut from the wreckage of their ship. It has been coloured for its appearance in this book. (Mary Evans Picture Library)

page 34 A sixteenth-century French sea-faring map of the world. Most of the scenes it depicts are purely imaginary. Notice how all the names to the north of the equator are written upside down. (Wayland Picture Library)

page 36 Sketches from Tasman's journal of his voyage through the Pacific, coloured for their appearance in this book. (Wayland Picture Library)

page 38 A painting by Australian artist G.W. Lambert (1873–1930) taken from an early twentieth-century book entitled *The Romance of Australia*. It shows Burke and Wills on their way to Mount Hopeless.

page 40 Photograph taken by Robert Peary during his last Arctic expedition of 1905, showing his five-man team standing at the North Pole. (Photo Research International)

page 42 One of the wonderful collection of photographs taken by Herbert Ponting (1870–1935) on Scott's second Antarctic expedition. His photographs of the Antarctic and other lonely corners of the earth are still some of the best ever taken in black-and-white. (Private collection)

page 44 An engraving (coloured for its appearance in this book) from *The Illu-strated London News* which was the first illustrated weekly journal. It began publication in 1842 and can still be bought today. This picture was drawn by an artist on the spot, then engraved on wood for printing. (Wayland Picture Library)

page 46 Another engraving from *The Illustrated London News*, coloured for this book. This time the scene is largely fanciful, and would have been drawn and engraved many months after the event depicted. (Wayland Picture Library)

page 48 A lithograph of a painting by Charles Tyrwhitt-Drake who accompanied Burton on his journey through Ethiopia. (The Photomas Index)

page 50 An eighteenth-century scroll painting of Lhasa's Potala Palace, from the Musée Guimet, Paris. (Michael Holford)

page 52 A black-and-white photograph taken from the Kon-Tiki's dinghy, subsequently hand-coloured for reproduction on slides and postcards. (The Kon-Tiki Museum, Oslo)

page 54 A colour photograph of Tenzing Norgay, taken by Edmund Hillary on the summit of Mount Everest in 1953. (Royal Geographical Society)

page 56 Photograph taken by Neil Armstrong in July 1969 on the surface of the moon. It shows Buz Aldrin standing beside seismic equipment. (Photo Research International)

Sources of Further Information

MUSEUMS

Every large town has a museum worth visiting because the subject of exploration covers so many interests. In London, for example, early navigational instruments can be found at the Science Museum. The National Maritime Museum has models of early ships, a Captain Cook wing, and thousands of paintings, prints, and books. At the National Portrait Gallery you may look at the faces of Ralegh, Drake, Cook, Scott, Shackleton, and many more. A town which boasts its own hero of exploration will probably have a museum, or part of a museum, devoted to him. In Oslo, for instance, there is a museum housing the *Fram* (Amundsen's polar exploration ship); the Kon-tiki Museum with the Kon-Tiki raft; and the Viking Ship Museum with three magnificent Viking ships.

There are no museums of exploration as such, but many museums have ancient maps and drawings, navigational instruments, primitive clothing, and other things which have a bearing on the subject. However, you would need guidance.

BOOKS

There are many books about particular explorers, which you should look for by name. For example, books about Marco Polo, Columbus, Drake, the Conquistadors, Lewis and Clark, Cook, Stanley, Burton, and Scott, can be found in every library. Books written by Stanley, several Australian explorers including John MacDouall Stuart, Burton, Heyerdahl, and Hillary exist in various editions. The *Encyclopedia Britannica* is a very good source of short biographies and accounts of voyages and land journeys.

Here are a few books about exploration in general:

Brading, Tilla, *Pirates and Buccaneers* (Wayland)

Grant, Neil, *Explorers* (Hamlyn)

Hewitt, James, *Famous Names in World Exploration* (Wayland)

Jenkins, Alan C. (Ed). *Exploration Earth* (Blackie)

Knight, Frank, *True Stories of Exploration* (Benn)

Monham, Kathleen, *Famous Names in Seafaring* (Wayland)

Finally, do not forget that there are thousands of books which, although not about exploration, have information on the subject. They include books on primitive peoples, history, science, natural history, and cartography. Of course, you would need a librarian to help you find the particular information you are seeking.

Glossary

Arabs: A race which originally inhabited Arabia and is now widely spread in western Asia and northern Africa.

astronaut: A person trained to travel in space.

circumnavigate: To sail completely round a piece of land, or round the whole world.

conquistadors: The Spanish conquerors of large parts of southern and central America in the sixteenth century.

Dutch East Indies Company: The company founded in the late sixteenth century to trade in the East Indies.

equator: The imaginary band round the earth which divides the northern and southern hemispheres, and which is equidistant from the poles.

Far East: A general term for the countries of eastern Asia, including China and Japan.

hemisphere: One half of the globe. There are north and south hemispheres, and east and west hemispheres.

estuary: The mouth of a river, which is subject to the sea's tides.

Indian: A native of India. However, natives of the American continent are also called Indians because of the belief of early explorers that they were in India.

Koran: The holy book of the Moslem religion.

Middle East: A general term for the countries of the eastern Mediterranean, especially the Arab countries.

Mongols: A race of eastern Asia which in the thirteenth century conquered most of Asia and eastern Europe.

Moslem: A follower of the religion created by Mahomet in the seventh century.

New World: The name given to the newly discovered American continent to distinguish it from the 'Old World' of Europe, Asia, and Africa.

North-East Passage: A route from the Atlantic to the Pacific, between the Arctic and the northern coast of Asia.

North Pole: The northernmost point of the earth.

North-West Passage: A route from the Atlantic to the Pacific, between the Arctic and the northern coast of Canada.

Ptolomey: Astronomer and geographer of second century who produced some of the earliest world maps, surprisingly accurate in some respects, wildly inaccurate in others.

Royal Geographical Society: The Society founded in London in the nineteenth century to promote the exploration of unknown places.

scurvy: A disease, eventually fatal, caused by lack of Vitamin C in the diet.

South Pole: The southernmost point of the earth.

Spice Islands: The Moluccas islands, and (loosely) some other islands of the East Indies, where most spices came from.

strait: A narrow passage of water connecting two large bodies of water.

Terra Australis Incognita: A vast continent supposed (until the eighteenth century) to exist in the southern hemisphere.

Index